photographs **Mick Hales**

text **Sandee Brawarsky**

introduction **David Hartman**

212 VIEWS OF CENTRAL PARK

EXPERIENCING NEW YORK CITY'S
JEWEL FROM EVERY ANGLE

STEWART, TABORI & CHANG

NEW YORK

Contents

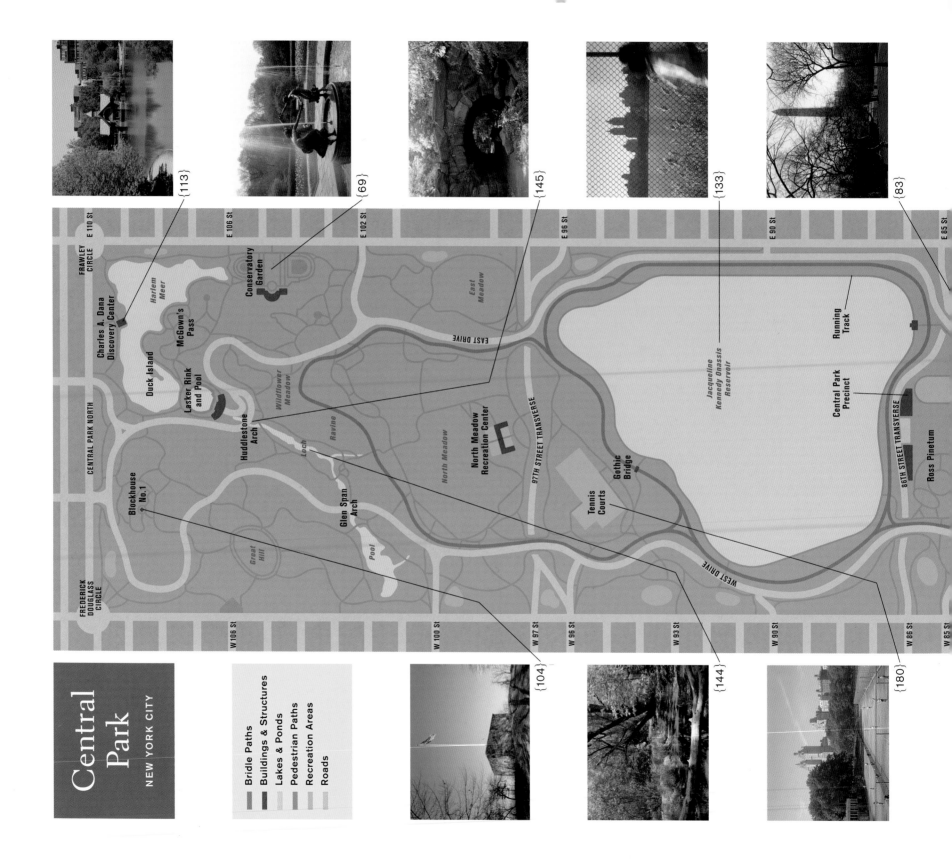

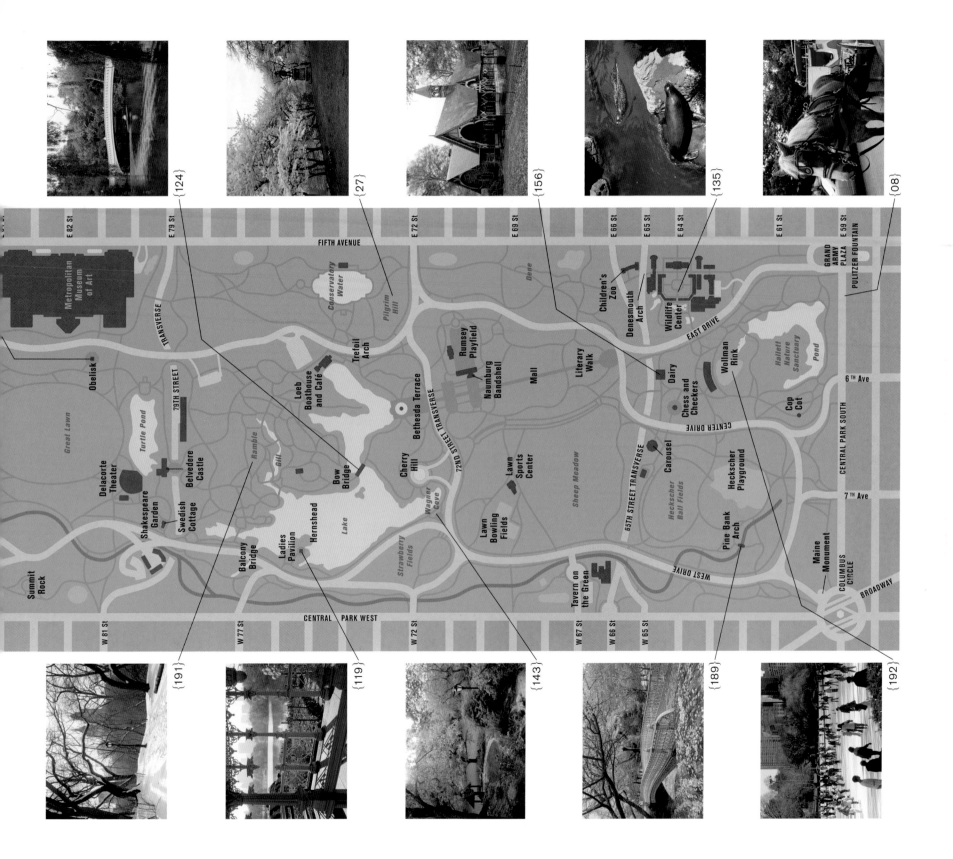

{124}

{27}

{156}

{135}

{08}

{191}

{119}

{143}

{189}

{192}

Metropolitan Museum of Art

E 82 St

E 79 St

FIFTH AVENUE

E 72 St

E 69 St

E 66 St

E 65 St

E 64 St

E 61 St

E 59 St

GRAND ARMY PLAZA

PULITZER FOUNTAIN

Conservatory Water

Pilgrim Hill

Dene

Children's Zoo

Denesmouth Arch

Wildlife Center

EAST DRIVE

TRANSVERSE

Obelisk

79TH STREET

Trefoil Arch

Rumsey Playfield

Naumburg Bandshell

Mall

Literary Walk

Dairy

Chess and Checkers

Wollman Rink

Hallett Nature Sanctuary

Pond

6TH Ave

Great Lawn

Turtle Pond

Loeb Boathouse and Café

Ramble

Gill

Bethesda Terrace

72ND STREET TRANSVERSE

Cop Cot

Delacorte Theater

Belvedere Castle

Bow Bridge

Cherry Hill

Lawn Sports Center

Sheep Meadow

65TH STREET TRANSVERSE

Carousel

Heckscher Playground

CENTER DRIVE

CENTRAL PARK SOUTH

Shakespeare Garden

Swedish Cottage

Hernshead

Lake

Wagner Cove

Lawn Bowling Fields

Heckscher Ball Fields

Pine Bank Arch

7TH Ave

Summit Rock

Balcony Bridge

Ladies Pavilion

Strawberry Fields

Tavern on the Green

WEST DRIVE

Maine Monument

COLUMBUS CIRCLE

BROADWAY

W 81 St

W 77 St

CENTRAL   PARK   WEST

W 72 St

W 67 St

W 66 St

W 65 St

Introduction

by David Hartman

OUR AMERICA IS A MIRACLE. NO OTHER NATION ON EARTH, EVER, HAS SO EMPOWERED its citizens to pretty much say what they want to say and try to become what they want to become without the powerful and the government telling them, "You can't do that!" The Constitution hovers over Americans, a protective umbrella of personal freedom and opportunity, guaranteeing that no matter our nationality, religion, or race we can go for it, try to make the most of our lives. And no city in America reflects that miracle more than New York, where millions of us, 365 days a year, live, work, and play together, bump into and yell at each other, and generally help one another survive and thrive.

There's another miracle within New York City, an 843-acre rectangle, an oasis where again, regardless of language, faith, or color, we can escape, temporarily, our volcanic lives. Most New Yorkers revel in the speed, noise, pressures, and energy of their city. But we also, occasionally, need to slow down, regroup, and energize ourselves to re-enter the fray. We come to Central Park.

{01} *Title page:* A path through the Ramble in winter.

{02} *Contents page:* Delphinium and early-summer perennials, along with other plants mentioned in Shakespeare's work, bloom alongside one of the many terraces in the Shakespeare Garden.

{03} *Opposite:* Bare trees look sculptural, with the Metropolitan Museum of Art as their backdrop.

This particular rectangle is a slice of vision and genius from America's first horticultural-ist, A. J. Downing, and poet-editor William Cullen Bryant. Some 150 years ago they inspired New York's politicians and community leaders to, as Bryant wrote, "rescue any part of [Manhattan] for health and recreation." In 1853 the New York State legislature authorized the creation of Central Park, which became a retreat from the foul air and cacophonous racket of the expanding city.

And a creation it was—almost entirely man-made. American landscape designer Frederick Law Olmsted and English architect Calvert Vaux led a team of brilliant artists and engineers in turning scrubby brush, rocky outcroppings, and stagnant swamps into a bucolic sanctuary, America's first landscaped urban park.

So, what is it about the Park that soothes and calms, not only New Yorkers, but millions of visitors from all over the world? Is it the ponds and pools, the bridle paths and ball fields, the world-class concerts and theater events, the fountains and gardens, the playgrounds and great lawns, the elm-canopied paths or the easy access to exercise and play? Or, that it's free?

All of the above.

Each of us has "our" Park. For some 12 years, most weekdays, I "ran" Central Park, along with roller bladers, bikers, people-strollers, and baby strollers; past the merry-go-round, muse-ums, and the Meer; past the arches, the bridges, and the boat pond, all the while hearing some languages I recognized and many that I didn't. For an hour each day I was surrounded by

thousands of strangers, each of them celebrating their own private moments as much as I.

Tony Bennett, the wonderful singer and artist, lives and paints overlooking the Park. He says, "Fall, especially, is a feast of color, chaotic beauty. The colors bang into each other and it all works."

Sarah Elliott, one of the many bird-watcher guides, says, "No matter how worried or depressed I might be, walking into the Park lifts my spirits. There's no way to leave this Park feeling worse than when you came in."

Barry Lewis, my partner in our New York City Walking Tour television programs for PBS says, "We had learned how to build cities, but Vaux and Olmsted taught us how to live in them. The Park civilizes us."

If you've never been to Central Park, do yourself a favor and go. It won't be your last visit. And if you cannot get there (or even if you can), your next best bet is to dive into this book. It's photographs and words will calm and soothe you, almost as if you were watching a red-tailed hawk soaring over the Sheep Meadow.

{08} *Top left:* For many New Yorkers, Central Park is their backyard, and the Sheep Meadow their lawn for sunbathing, exercising, and relaxing.

{09} *Top right:* The Bethesda Terrace, with the Ramble in the background, is one of the classic settings for Park portraits, both formal and informal.

{10} *Bottom left:* Roller skaters moving along the Park drives at a fast clip get a cinematic view of the Park's landscape.

{11} *Bottom right:* Schools and community groups utilize the Park's ball fields for practice and games.

Forward and Back

{12-36}

Central Park grew into its name. When it was planned and built in the 1850s, the park was located on what was then the northern edge of Manhattan. Its planners wisely envisioned the city's rapid growth and assumed that it would ultimately surround the Park. But the name is more than just geographic; Central Park is essential. It's New York's heart; its winding roads pulse with the city's lifeblood. New York City without Central Park is unthinkable.

In the 1840s, a group of civic-minded New Yorkers advanced the idea of building a major public park in the tradition of the great parks of European cities. They believed that the timing was urgent, that before too long every inch of land would be covered with roads and buildings. Among the major advocates of America's first landscaped public park were poet and editor William Cullen Bryant, landscape architect Andrew Jackson Downing, and writer Washington Irving. At first, officials favored a site near the East River, but they ended up selecting the land that is now Central Park and in 1853 the State Legislature passed a bill authorizing its acquisition. In 1856 the Central Park Commission was created to plan and manage the new Park.

{12} *Opposite:* Patches of daffodils in early spring, when the Park is full of radiant bursts of color.

{13} *Left:* A snow-covered landscape near West 77th Street, with Balcony Bridge in the background.

{14} *Right:* The Conservatory Garden's southern garden, with its mix of shrubs, trees, and flowers, surrounding Bessie Potter Vonnoh's sculpture.

{15} *Opposite:* Stately elm trees arranged in straight rows alongside the Mall. In the Park's early days, goat-cart rides for children ran up and down the Mall.

One of the facts about Central Park that surprises many visitors is that it's man-made: the lakes are constructed, the waterfalls dependent on piped-in water, and the trees—more than 26,000 of them—were all planted. This plot of land was a canvas for the imaginative and enduring work of its designers, Frederick Law Olmsted and Calvert Vaux. Before the area became Central Park, it was hardly scenic, filled with swamps and rocky outcrops. And it was home to about 1,600 people, among them immigrant farmers, gardeners, tradespeople, and squatters. In the northeast section of the Park, an order of Catholic nuns, the Sisters of Charity, ran a complex of buildings that included a convent, a chapel, and two schools.

On the west side of what is now the Park, what may have been Manhattan's first prominent community of African-American property owners flourished in a settlement called Seneca Village. A historical marker in the West 80s now commemorates the site where more than 250 people lived, founded a school and three churches, and set up burial grounds. Park authorities compensated those who owned or leased property when they

{16} King Wladyslaw Jagiello is depicted with two swords crossed above his head, symbolizing the union of the Polish and Lithuanian troops he led in battle. The bronze equestrian statue overlooking the Turtle Pond was originally featured at the Polish pavilion at the New York World's Fair of 1939–1940 and donated to the Park in 1945.

were displaced, although many contested the settlement amounts.

By 1857, workers were clearing the land that stretched from 59th to 106th Streets, and from Fifth to Eighth Avenues. (In 1863 the Park was extended to 110th Street, bringing it to its present 843 acres.) There was little earth-moving machinery then, and in order to move mountains or create them, workers had to rely on pure manpower and horsepower. In a monumental effort, they drained swamps, removed huge amounts of stone and topsoil, and blasted through Manhattan schist, the major bedrock of the island, to transform the rectangle of rocky marshland into a picturesque landscape.

A national competition was held for the best design for Central Park, and in 1858, the Greensward Plan, submitted by Olmsted and Vaux, was selected. Olmsted, who had worked as a farmer and a journalist and was known for his reporting on the American South, was then Superintendent of Central Park. Vaux was an architect who had been a partner and protégé of Andrew Downing. Olmsted's great familiarity with Central Park

{17} *Left:* A horse-and-buggy driver, dressed for a day in the country, points out some sights to his passengers. Many of the drivers are knowledgeable tour guides who love the Park.

{18} *Right:* The Maine Monument honors the memory of 258 American sailors who were killed when the battleship Maine exploded in the harbor of Havana, Cuba, in 1898.

{19} *Left:* Intricately detailed but fragile sandstone carvings of birds and wildlife at Bethesda Terrace.

{20} *Right:* Bethesda Terrace, here undergoing some minor repairs, was the only formal element included in the original Greensward Plan.

{21} *Opposite:* A framed view of the centerpiece of Bethesda Terrace, Emma Stebbins's *Angel of the Waters.*

and Vaux's great knowledge of landscape gardening helped them to create a plan that was both practical and poetic. Conceived as a whole, it suggested a sculpted country setting in the English naturalist tradition, with pleasingly varied terrain—a Manhattan Arcadia. Through innovative design elements, the designers realized their ideal of the Park as a refuge, an island of tranquility amidst the commotion and confinement of the streets of New York.

Olmsted was named Architect-in-Chief, and Vaux became his assistant. The two men shared a vision of how the Park would look and a belief in the democratic spirit that would inform it: they saw this as a park for all New Yorkers. In their report they wrote, "It is one great purpose of the Park to supply to the hundreds of thousands of tired workers, who have no opportunity to spend their summers in the country, a specimen of God's handiwork that shall be to them, inexpensively, what a month or two in the White Mountains or the Adirondacks is, at great cost, to those in easier circumstances."

The talents of Olmsted and Vaux were complementary, although Vaux's accomplishments have been large-ly overshadowed by Olmsted's. Chief gardener Ignatz Pilat and architect Jacob Wrey Mould, along with engi-neers George Waring and William Grant, were also intricately involved in bringing the Greensward Plan for Central Park to life. Olmsted and Vaux were both involved with the Park for many years, minus a couple of intervals when they resigned over disagreements with the Park's Board of Commissioners. Olmsted left for good in 1878; Vaux remained involved until his death in 1895. The pair also designed other parks, including Brooklyn's Prospect Park.

The first tree in Central Park was planted on October 17, 1858. The Park opened officially to the public in the winter of 1858-59. One of the most popular features was the Lake, a lovely, bucolic spot transformed from a swamp, where people could ice-skate. On Sundays when the Lake was frozen over, thousands of skaters, novice and expert alike, came to the Park; they looked for a red ball, raised over Vista Rock, to signal that the

{22} *Opposite:* In the early days of the Park, the Sheep Meadow was a grazing area for the 150 sheep who slept in the nearby sheepfold; they were ban-ished in 1934.

{23} *Left:* A running track surrounds the Reservoir, which was completed in 1862 while the Park was being constructed.

{24} *Right:* The Victorian-style Ladies' Pavilion looks out onto the Lake.

{25} *Left:* Rowboats are available for hire on the Lake.

{26} *Right:* The Wollman Rink, at the southern end of the Park, was opened in 1949.

{27} *Opposite:* John Quincy Adams Ward's *The Pilgrim* stands amidst cherry trees, looking west, his musket ready.

Lake was open. In old photos and illustrations, pairs of skaters glide on the ice, exuberantly, sometimes with their children alongside.

In warmer weather, there were open-air concerts and carriage parades. The Carousel and other attractions were added later, and for many years the Park was a work in progress. After Olmsted and Vaux, others left their mark on Central Park. The original designers were not in favor of having statues in the Park, but there was much interest, particularly among immigrant groups, in donating commemorative sculptures and monuments, and there are now more than fifty sculptures and monuments in the Park. Several planned projects never came to be; the idea of a racetrack on the west side, for example, had some official support in the 1890s, but was ultimately defeated.

Robert Moses, who was Parks Commissioner from 1934 to 1960, left a significant imprint on Central Park, as well as on the general landscape of the metropolitan area. He was responsible for adding new parks and

beaches, as well as a network of parkways, bridges, public housing, and major public works projects. In Central Park, he added many playgrounds and the Wollman Skating Rink; created a full roster of sports activities, tournaments, and festivals; renovated the Zoo; and tore down the Casino, an elegant restaurant on what is now the site of Rumsey Playfield. He built the Tavern on the Green restaurant on what had been a sheepfold, and did significant reconstruction work throughout the Park. Not necessarily guided by the pastoral aims of the Greensward Plan, Moses made changes and repairs grounded in practicality and the promotion of recreational activities.

By the 1970s, the Park was suffering from decades of overuse, neglect, and natural decay; the place that earlier had had more shades of green than anywhere in New York was fading. Funding from the City for the Park's upkeep and maintenance fell far short of its needs. Fortunately, a Park champion emerged: Elizabeth Barlow (now Elizabeth Barlow Rogers), a city planner with a special interest in parks, was named Central Park

{28} *Opposite:* The Lake, here frozen over, was carved out of swampland.

{29} *Left:* One of the arabesque-style staircase panels at Bethesda Terrace depicting the seasons.

{30} *Right:* To the tune of nursery rhymes played at half-hour intervals, the bronze animals whimsically glide around the tower of the Delacorte Clock, near the entrance to the Zoo.

 Left: **A statue of William Shakespeare, the work of John Quincy Adams Ward, stands at the beginning of Literary Walk, near the Mall.**

{32} *Right:* **A view from Bow Bridge at dusk.**

{33} *Opposite:* **A cluster of azaleas that come to bloom in early May adds vibrant color to the southernmost section of the Dene, a stretch of pastoral landscape near the Park's East 60s edge.**

Administrator in 1979, and in 1980 she and others founded the Central Park Conservancy to raise funds for the Park and develop a master plan for its restoration and ongoing maintenance in keeping with the naturalist vision of Olmstead and Vaux. Since then, in partnership with the Parks Department, the Central Park Conservancy has been responsible for major projects throughout the Park.

As Douglas Blonsky, Central Park Administrator and Chief Operating Officer of the Central Park Conservancy, says, "There's still a lot more work to do; there are always new projects." Throughout the year, the Park's gardeners and maintenance crews are cleaning, pruning, re-seeding, planting, and generally keeping watch over the Park. Other staff members and volunteers offer walking tours, athletic programs, educational projects, and distribute Park information. It takes a village, so to speak, to operate the Park. Upstairs at the Arsenal—one of two Park buildings that predate Olmsted and Vaux—in the offices of the Parks Department, the original Greensward Plan is available for viewing. The fortress-like Arsenal was built by New York State

{34} Belvedere Castle is an example of the eclectic architectural styles favored by Vaux, who designed the stone structure.

between 1847 and 1851 as a munition storehouse, and over the years it has housed a police precinct, Zoo animals, and even the Museum of Natural History. Its second-floor library, open to the public, features an interesting selection of books on New York history and Park history, along with specialized volumes of Central Park tree inventories.

Some of the books feature nineteenth-century photographs and Currier & Ives engravings of Central Park. These images reveal a landscape that is largely unchanged today. Details such as automobiles, clothing styles, and the social customs depicted are different of course. But it's not hard to imagine the Park in its early days while strolling through it today. One way to time-travel to the past is to take a tour in a horse-drawn carriage, focusing on the clip-clop sound of the hooves, looking straight ahead into the Park and avoiding a view of the skyscrapers surrounding it. The tableau of trees, grass, and rocks on gently contoured land is timeless.

{35} *Left:* A detail of the cast-iron latticework on Pine Bank Arch.

{36} *Right:* Olmsted and Vaux considered the red-brick Arsenal with Norman-style towers to be an eyesore, so they planted trees around it that would grow large enough to provide a screen.

Crossings
{37-61}

Enter Central Park and everything changes. There are no fire escapes, cash machines, subway grates, parking meters; none of Manhattan's urban street scenery. Trees and winding pathways are visible just inside, creating a chain of linked panoramas. The light is almost tangible, whether bouncing off the mica-laced rocks, shining through lush foliage, or illuminating bare-branch silhouettes. On sunny mornings, the blue sky seems enormous.

The Park is a pause in a city defined by its hectic motion and nonstop beat; it's a whisper to Manhattan's roar. Whether people are passing through the Park to get to the other side, ambling without purpose, or using it as their gym, they would surely agree that it has an airiness rarely encountered elsewhere in the city. Even footsteps sound different on its hexagonal asphalt blocks or paved paths.

"When I get 150 yards into Central Park, I feel like I'm in the country," an Irish carriage driver from County Kerry remarks, inhaling a great breath of air as he crosses the border from city to park. He likes to sit sideways, facing his passengers while directing his horse around the lower loop, so that he can take in the whole view at once.

{37} *Opposite:* In the Conservatory Garden, two identical walkways, or allées, lined with flowering crab apple trees separate the central, formal Italian-style garden from the adjacent English-style and French-style gardens.

{38} *Left:* From Columbus Circle at 59th Street, a view of the towering Maine monument that stands at Merchant's Gate, the Park entrance at the southwest corner.

{39} *Right:* This figure, and another on the opposite side of the Maine Monument, represent the Pacific and Atlantic Oceans, symbolizing the vastness of the American continent.

Separating the Park from the city is a pyramid-topped stone wall, low enough so that passersby can glimpse the wooded landscape on the other side. Every few blocks, a break in the wall forms a simple entrance. Of the more than fifty entrances to the Park, twenty have names that hint at interesting stories; Scholars' Gate, at 60th Street and Fifth Avenue; Strangers' Gate, at 106th Street and Central Park West; and Pioneers' Gate, at 110th Street and Fifth Avenue, among others. Although these names are carved into the stone, few people know them, or even that the gates have names.

When the Park was nearing its final stages of completion, after Olmsted and Vaux had resigned as the Park's landscape architects in 1863 (to later return), several members of the Park's Board of Commissioners sought to build elaborate gates with ornate ironwork, statues, and pedestals, at the entranceways on Central Park South, as a way to mark the successful completion of the Park. As historians Roy Rosenzweig and Elizabeth Blackmar explain in *The Park and the People*, it was Vaux who convinced the authorities to abandon

{40} Here along Central Park South, the perimeter wall forms a boundary between urban and pastoral worlds, between pavement and earth.

the idea, which was not in the democratic spirit of the Greensward Plan. Today, however, there is one grand, wrought-iron gate to the Park; the Vanderbilt Gate, at the entrance to the Conservatory Garden. Once part of the family's Fifth Avenue mansion, it was presented to the Park in 1939.

The perimeter wall is interrupted for several blocks by the Metropolitan Museum of Art, not a Park building, but the largest structure in the Park. Perhaps one of the most striking images of transition between city and park is the Museum's back wall. Running up its white stone surface is a spreading growth of ivy, and the cluster of nearby trees is reflected in its wall of windows.

Across Central Park South, Fifth Avenue, 110th Street and Central Park West, a ring of apartment buildings, hotels, and museums forms a kind of rampart around it. After dark, their lighted windows create a checkerboard backdrop behind the trees. The doormen whose buildings face Central Park have a perpetual view of Olmsted and Vaux's creation. "I see every change," a cheerful gentleman says, while standing outside

{41} *Opposite:* Forsythia conceal the East Drive, which the Trefoil Arch passes under. Designed by Vaux and Mould, it was completed in 1862.

{42} *Left:* The windowed back wall of the Metropolitan Museum of Art becomes a mirror to a row of trees.

{43} *Right:* Made in France, the Vanderbilt Gate, at 105th Street and Fifth Avenue, leads to the Conservatory Garden, the most formal garden in the Park.

{44} *Left:* A doorman at the San Remo on Central Park West has a close-up view of the Park.

{45} *Right:* Drivers park their horses and carriages, waiting for fares, along Central Park South. Through the late 1800s, carriages were the sole travelers on the Carriage Drive that loops around the Park.

the building he serves on upper Fifth Avenue. "I watch the leaves falling, I notice the winds. When I can see all the way across to Central Park West, I know it's cold." Pointing to the trees directly in front of him, he adds with satisfaction, "That's my little piece of the Park."

On the opposite edge, just inside the Women's Gate on Central Park West at 72nd Street, a late-morning New York minute passes: I count two joggers, three women with strollers, one man in a business suit and sneakers, one bicyclist, and two power walkers entering the Park. Soon after, a young man holding the tangled leashes of two small dogs follows them in, with a fellow on roller skates close behind. A woman with a crumpled newspaper heads for a seat in the shaded pergola. Three tourists with cameras and guidebooks ask a hot dog vendor for directions to Strawberry Fields. A group of schoolchildren waving clipboards bursts in, engaged in a nature assignment. This is typical traffic, according to the top-hatted doorman who stands outside of Tavern on the Green, a few blocks to the south, and has a sweeping view northeast into the Park. He says there's

{46} The vendor sells hot dogs, soft pretzels, drinks and more throughout the year, stationed at a busy crossroads between the West Drive and a footpath along the north end of the Sheep Meadow. The stately ginkgo tree provides welcome shade.

hardly a moment during his shift when not one person is crossing into the Park.

Walking around the Park, or cutting through it, requires making choices. A system of three separate pathways—the carriage road, the footpath, and the bridle path—circumnavigates the entire huge rectangle. In a very different pattern from the city's strict horizontal/vertical grid of streets, all of the pathways curve and twist, often leading to unexpected vistas, like when a cascading waterway suddenly comes into view in the Ravine, at the northern end of the Park. Following any of the pathways allows for uninterrupted travel. When the different paths intersect, a handsome bridge or arch offers a crossing. Each of the Park's thirty-six spans is distinctive. While crossing an arch or bridge provides an overlook, passing underneath one of them offers artful moments too: the intrados, the arch's inner rim, becomes a framing device for the view ahead, even as it shifts. Traveling through the archways that tunnel underneath the East and West Drives, many walkers find it irresistible to shout out, "Hello!" The Park always answers.

{47} *Opposite:* An exit from the East Drive, bordered with maple, oak, linden, and cherry trees leads out of the Park onto East 72nd Street.

{48} *Left:* Rhythmic dancers practice their art across from the Park on the Fifth Avenue side of the Pulitzer fountain.

{49} *Right:* Near the 67th Street entrance, a doorman stands on duty outside of Tavern on the Green, which opened in 1934.

{50} *Left:* Taxis share the Park Drive—which used to be known as the Carriage Drive—with cars, horse-drawn carriages, bicyclists, runners, and skaters.

{51} *Right:* Many of the Park's walkways are lined with benches, some modeled after those designed for the 1939 New York World's Fair.

{52} *Opposite:* Flowering cherry trees at the base of Pilgrim Hill overlook Park Drive.

Concealed by trees and shrubbery, the four transverse roads that link the East and West Sides of Manhattan rarely intrude on the sense of tranquility Park visitors enjoy. One of many examples of the ingeniousness of Olmsted and Vaux's Greensward Plan, the transverse roads—at 65th, 79th, 86th and 96th Streets—dip below the level of the Park, and traffic sounds are muted. A walker on the southern edge of the Sheep Meadow, near 65th Street, is probably unaware of being within yards of a city bus line. But travelers on these roadways feel their exclusion. A veteran taxi driver and Park lover affirms the efficiency of the transverse roads in getting across town. "But you don't get to see the Park," he laments. "Only the stones." He takes the surface-level, interior East and West Drives, going north or south, whenever he can.

There's nothing haphazard about Central Park's design. Olmsted and Vaux deliberately created distinct types of landscape: the pastoral, which is airy and open; the picturesque, less ordered and more mysterious, a bit of wild nature; and the formal areas, where nature is most tamed and built upon. Think Thomas

Gainsborough's English countrysides, Thomas Cole's forest landscapes, and Georges Seurat's *La Grande Jatte;* they flow freely, from one into another.

Whether they are standing at the edge of an open field, in dense clusters, or in strict geometric order, the trees guide you in moving from one kind of space into another. Along the Mall, in a flat, grassy area with low, cast-iron fences adjacent to the paved walk, majestic elms, probably the Park's only straight line of trees, rise in double rows. Their trunks form an orderly margin for the formal lane, while the branches create a broad and beautiful canopy overhead. This wide walkway runs on a diagonal to the Park's rectangle, leading from Literary Walk to Bethesda Terrace, the main formal area of the Park. As walkers approach the Terrace, the Bethesda Fountain, and the Lake from the south, the wooded hills of the Ramble gradually come into view. Further along on the same diagonal line of vision is Vista Rock and its crown, Belvedere Castle.

It's easy to get turned around and lose your bearings in the Park, but re-orienting is simple; just look for

{53} *Opposite:* Adjacent to the Mall, the Park's elm trees comprise one of the largest stands of American elms in the country.

{54} *Left:* Mature elm trees, like these, usually reach heights of sixty to eighty feet.

{55} *Right:* Trees frame the edge of the Sheep Meadow, here a sea of green.

{56} *Left:* An elegant cast-iron luminaire, an art nouveau-style lamppost, one of several styles of Central Park lights.

{57} *Right:* Joggers pass the stairway leading to Bethesda Terrace as they cross the lower loop of the Park Drive at 72nd Street, also known as Terrace Drive.

{58} *Opposite:* A rustic pergola near the 72nd Street entrance, with a luminaire in the background.

the skyline beyond the Park's boundaries. Park regulars use familiar landmarks like the Dakota apartment building on West 72nd Street, or the Plaza Hotel on 59th Street, as their compass points. And throughout the Park, in the Ramble as well as around the ball fields, lamposts are a source of invaluable information. Most are numbered, and the first two digits refer to the nearest cross street. (A lamppost numbered 8503, for instance, would be near 85th Street.)

The Park is, of course, free to all. A ticket seller at the Zoo says that occasionally tourists pay for tickets at her booth and then keep walking, headed toward the parallel archway to the Denesmouth Arch, which supports the 65th Street transverse. She dashes out to direct them back toward the Zoo and learns that they weren't planning on going to the Zoo at all, but thought that they needed to pay before going under the Arch. Like a Central Park ambassador, she explains that entering the bucolic expanse ahead requires no fee—that all this pleasing scenery is a gift to and from the City of New York.

{59} *Opposite:* The circular concourse atop Cherry Hill, with its central Victorian fountain, was a popular gathering place in the 19th century for visitors on horseback or in carriages.

{60} *Left:* The approach to the 65th Street transverse runs on top of this arch, near the entrance to the Children's Zoo and the Denesmouth Arch.

{61} *Right:* A classical sculpture in honor of architect Richard Morris Hunt, erected in 1898, interrupts the perimeter wall on Fifth Avenue near 71st Street.

Rooted in Place

{62-86}

A YOUNG WOMAN SPORTS A DOWN JACKET OVER HER WEDDING GOWN. IT'S A WINTER DAY AT CENTRAL Park's Bethesda Terrace, with temperatures near freezing. The bride is surrounded by eleven men wearing black pants and white jackets, and a group of ten women huddling together in pale blue dresses. The center of attention, the bride takes off her coat and, in her sleeveless flounce of a dress, smiling for a photographer, poses in the locked gaze of her husband-to-be, Bethesda Fountain behind them. When asked why she chose this spot on such a cold day, she answers in accented English, teeth chattering, "This is the most beautiful place in New York."

Bethesda Terrace is indeed a spectacular backdrop and also a rich foreground; it's one of many Park sites that makes a strong impression on the twenty million visitors who come through the Park every year. Each of these sites is a small world, an aesthetic pleasure, a place to drink in slowly. Designed with sensitivity to integrate the man-made and natural worlds, these are places that engage the senses as well as the imagination. They're popular destinations for people-watching, sketching the scenery, reading newspapers, or wandering about.

{62} *Opposite:* With water lilies floating nearby in a reflecting pool in the Conservatory Garden, Bessie Potter Vonnoh's bronze sculpture, installed in 1936, honors Frances Hodgson Burnett, author of *The Secret Garden.*

If Central Park were a kingdom, Belvedere Castle might be the main address, but Bethesda Terrace would be the royal court. With its elegant double staircase and seven arches leading underneath the Terrace Bridge, Bethesda Terrace, designed by Calvert Vaux, is the grandest place in the Park. The balustrades and end posts, designed by Jacob Wrey Mould, are intricately decorated with sculpted details. A restored portion of the high ceiling of the arcade under the bridge hints at its former glory, with colorful glazed tiles arranged in an arabesque pattern. A street performer named Thoth, who likes to play his violin and sing in the tunnel, calls it his temple.

Many Park paths wind their way to the Terrace. Often, birds perch on the wings of *Angel of the Waters*, the fountain centerpiece. The only sculpture that was part of the original plan, this work by Emma Stebbins commemorates the bringing of fresh water into New York City from the Croton Aqueduct, which opened in 1842. On late Saturday afternoons in the summer, a group of tango aficionados meet, supplying their own recorded

{63} *Opposite:* Vaux referred to Bethesda Terrace as the "Park's drawing room."

{64} *Left:* The arcade underneath Bethesda Bridge is itself a beautiful space, leading out onto the Lower Terrace.

{65} *Right:* A carved owl and bat on one side of an end post represents night; on the other sides are carvings of a book and lamp, and a witch and pumpkin. Its parallel end post features symbols of day.

{66} *Left:* Emma Stebbins's sculpture, *Angel of the Waters*, at the center of Bethesda Fountain, was dedicated in 1873.

{67} *Right:* Thoth, seen here in full costume and lively motion, is the subject of an Oscar-winning film. He performs regularly in the Bethesda Fountain tunnel.

{68} *Opposite:* Winter twilight at Bethesda Terrace, one of the first structures built in the Park, completed in 1864.

Latin music; the brick plaza adjacent to the *Angel* becomes their dance floor.

Toward the northeast end of the Park, the formal Conservatory Garden is another work of art, with its manicured greenery, perennials, and wildflowers, all in a brilliant color scheme. Even in November, a few deep-pink Carefree Winds roses still cling to their stems. The Garden's name reflects the history of the site: although not part of the Greensward Plan, a glass conservatory for showcasing elaborate floral exhibits was built here around the turn of the twentieth century, and was torn down in 1934. The current Garden was constructed as part of a Works Project Administration effort, set in motion by Robert Moses, and opened in 1937.

In the northernmost section, which is a French-style garden, with its circular flower beds ringing a central fountain, three schoolgirls in uniform report that they play there every afternoon. Best friends, they enjoy racing around the fountain, and when they catch each other and join hands, for a fleeting moment they resemble the figures in Walter Schott's sculpture *Three Dancing Maidens*. In spring, thousands of tulips bloom;

in the fall they are replaced by chrysanthemums. Every day, there's something new to see, and after a rain the garden shimmers.

South of the French garden is a more formal Italian-style garden with a broad lawn, and beyond that an English-style garden filled with a variety of flowers, trees, and shrubs; each garden has a fountain. Separating the three are double rows, or allées, of crab apple trees, whose pink and white blossoms seem, at their peak, to float on the branches. White-jacketed staff members from the hospital across Fifth Avenue eat lunch on the benches, and a woman reads to an elderly gentleman in a wheelchair, his face turned toward the flowers and the sun. The Conservatory Garden is also a popular place for weddings and wedding portraits; one couple doesn't seem to mind at all when a class of admiring first-graders gets into the photos.

To the south and west, set into the hill leading up to Belvedere Castle, the Shakespeare Garden is a literary as well as a visual pleasure. The poppies, asters, roses, daffodils, raspberries, holly, columbine, and a wealth

{69} *Opposite:* The Untermyer Fountain, with Walter Schott's bronze sculpture, *Three Dancing Maidens.*

{70} *Left:* Around the fountain, beds of flowers create patterns in the French-style garden.

{71} *Right:* A thick row of tulips is the outermost ring of the northern garden, surrounding the fountain and the inner circle of flowers.

{72} *Top left:* A bed of red hollyhocks growing in the Shakespeare Garden.

{73} *Bottom left:* The Garden was dedicated to Shakespeare in 1916, three hundred years after his death.

{74} *Right:* A sundial surrounded by greenery in the Shakespeare Garden.

{75} *Opposite:* Petals and splashes of sunlight look like snow along this lane.

of other flowers and plants that bloom in the terraced Garden are all mentioned in the Bard's plays and poems. Some plants have bronze plaques nearby quoting the relevant lines from Shakespeare's work. According to legend, the white mulberry tree grew from a cutting taken from Stratford-on-Avon, where Shakespeare was born and is buried. Nearby, at the Park's open-air Delacorte Theater, the New York Shakespeare Festival presents free summertime plays and musicals, inaugurated by the late Joseph Papp in 1957 and featuring leading Broadway and film actors. The Turtle Pond and Vista Rock are backdrops for all productions. Lines for the free tickets form early in the day and wind around the Great Lawn.

The Garden began in 1913 as a Victorian-style rock garden, was replanted and dedicated to Shakespeare in 1916, and was restored and rededicated in the late 1980s. Although the arrangements in this informal garden look as though they might be random, the plants are carefully placed according to color and blooming time, making for a resplendent spring and summer. Visitors tend to slow down their New York pace on the

fieldstone walkways alongside the flowers, as though perfecting the art of noticing. A fence made of tree branches encircles the Garden, and a few benches in the same style offer nooks for reading in this designated quiet zone.

All of the Park's gardens are tended with great care. Central Park is divided into forty-nine zones, and each zone has a team of gardeners responsible for it. Central Park Administrator Douglas Blonsky says that the team members are like ambassadors for their area. Over the years, they've added to the gardens and enhanced them, understanding the patterns of growth, shade, the play of the skyline, and the special challenges of gardening in the middle of the city. These gardens have come to feel like sacred places.

North of the Shakespeare Garden, on the opposite end of the Great Lawn, an alcove of evergreen trees called the Arthur Ross Pinetum is bathed in a distinctive light. Although there are evergreens throughout the Park, here the many varieties are concentrated. This international array of hundreds of pine trees, including

{76} *Opposite:* In simple, classic style, the Conservatory's central or Italian garden features a lush lawn and a single-jet fountain.

{77} *Left:* The walkways and flowers of the Conservatory Garden are a surprise discovery to many New Yorkers as well as out-of-town visitors.

{78} *Right:* The formal arrangements in the Conservatory Garden contrast with the Park's more naturalistic elements.

{79} *Left:* The Conservatory Garden offers four seasons of striking color, texture and fragrance.

{80} *Right:* Major renovation efforts in the Conservatory Garden by the Central Park Conservancy have had splendid results.

{81} *Opposite:* Azaleas and other plants surround the plaza at Cherry Hill, now a popular place for beginning roller skaters.

the Japanese White, Himalayan, Weeping White, and Swiss Stone pines, looks particularly striking when there's a fresh cover of snow. Even without snow, the dense green of the Pinetum is a refreshing sight in winter. It's a richly sensuous experience to walk through here, breathing in the aromas, or reaching out to touch the needles, some stiff and some silky; and walking on the ground cushioned by fallen needles, offers a pleasant contrast for feet accustomed to pounding city pavement. Most of the pine trees are pyramid-shaped, with varying amounts of trunk showing at the bottom, as if they're wearing dresses of different lengths. A line from James Russell Lowell's 1848 poem, "The pine is the mother of legends," captures the mythical feel of this place.

Southeast of the Pinetum, a man-made object with a history much older than the Park inspires a different kind of awe. A four-sided, pink granite pillar inscribed with hieroglyphics, the Obelisk was erected about 3,500 years ago in Egypt by Thothmes III. Now ensconced in Gotham—and most often referred to by its nickname, "Cleopatra's Needle," as in a song from Leonard Bernstein's "On the Town"—the towering stone is

{82} The Obelisk was built in 1443 B.C. as one of a pair of tapered columns in the Egyptian city of On, called Heliopolis by the Greeks, and later shipped to Alexandria.

surrounded by a plaza in Greywacke Knoll, between the Metropolitan Museum of Art and the Great Lawn.

To look at this pillar, more than 70 feet high, and weighing more than 200 tons, is to marvel at its construction, and also its journey to New York. It took 38 days to transport the Obelisk from Alexandria to New York by ship, and then 144 days to get it from the Hudson River to Central Park. When it was set in place on January 22, 1881, a crowd of more than 10,000 people came out to cheer. It still draws many visitors. A plaque at its base translates the writing, which tells of Ra and Rameses. At the four corners bronze crabs, each weighing more than 900 pounds, support the structure.

"It inspires me," a saxophone player says of the Obelisk, filling the air with music that incorporates ancient scales and Middle Eastern melodies. "I'm practicing here to get a feel for it," he says, showing his handwritten sheet music. When he was a child, his mother would take him to the Metropolitan Museum of Art, where he developed an interest in things Egyptian. The Obelisk, he says, "makes me feel powerful, strong, positive."

{83} *Left:* The Obelisk, set in a quiet, landscaped area, is the largest outdoor antiquity in New York City, and one of the best-known monuments in the Park.

{84} *Right:* Robert Graham's bronze sculpture of Duke Ellington, at the northeast corner of the Park, was dedicated in 1997.

{85} *Opposite:* Steps at the back of the Conservatory's central garden lead up to a terrace with a wrought-iron pergola, entwined with wisteria branches; in May the purple blossoms are profuse.

{86} *This page:* The central garden's geyser, set against the skyline at the northeastern end of the Park.

Overlooks
{87-111}

Some Central Park views are finest in their unfolding. Walkers coming around the bend at about 103rd Street, heading south on the West Drive, find that they're climbing slightly upward. Slowly, the water in the Reservoir comes into sight, with the buildings on the south and east sides of the Park also rising into full view like a garden wall to the Park's expanse. Within moments, water, sky, skyscrapers, and in spring, pink cherry blossoms, are visible ahead.

Call it the panoramic instinct or the city dweller's yearning for expansive views. Olmsted and Vaux had it right: they understood that Park visitors would enjoy seeing nature up close and would also thrill in over-looking it from a distance. They were composing these views at a time when re-creating natural scenery through stereoscopic photography was growing in popularity. Viewers would look at cards with dual images through a special viewer called a stereoscope; the two images would fuse into one, bringing a scene into three dimensions, as though the viewer were standing in the foreground. Visiting Central Park brought that stereo-scopic experience to life.

{87} *Opposite:* From a rooftop on Central Park South, the Park is a stripe of foliage in the midst of the city; here, it's a showcase of fall colors.

Many points of high elevation in Central Park could be described as a "belvedere," the Italian word for a structure with a beautiful view, and the name of the castle Olmsted and Vaux built. Designed by Vaux, Belvedere Castle was completed in 1867. When broadcasters announce the weather in Central Park, the Castle is their source of information. Since 1919, it has been a data-collecting station for the U.S. Weather Bureau. Now it also serves as an information and educational center where kids can learn about the natural world through hands-on study. At night it's a popular spot for stargazing. In the early mornings, a bird-watching group gathers on the terrace before a walk; in the fall, it's a good place to see migrating hawks.

Inside Belvedere Castle, the narrow staircase leads to lookouts from the tower as well as from its upper terrace. Facing north, you'll see ducks in the Turtle Pond and behind that, the expanse of the Great Lawn, formerly the site of a reservoir that was drained in 1930. On a summer afternoon, the Great Lawn is crowded with softball games. But deep into each outfield and removed from the baselines, families picnic, kids fly kites, and

gymnasts practice handsprings and flips. From the Castle's terrace you can see skylines on both the east and west sides of the city. At dusk, the sunset leaves traces of pink behind the American Museum of Natural History, right across from the Park at 79th Street.

Peering up at Belvedere Castle from the wooden pier that juts into Turtle Pond, the rugged, ash-gray stone structure looks as if it's rising out of Vista Rock, a huge mass of Manhattan schist. It's an eclectic, asymmetrical castle, a Moorish-Gothic-Norman-style fortress of a building, with a bit of the whimsical, too. The two pavilions, with their painted accents of yellow, terra cotta, and blue-gray, add a colorful touch. In the fog, the Castle is particularly magical; the mist envelops Manhattan's own little Camelot.

Not quite castles, three wooden shelters, built atop huge rock outcroppings—the Summerhouse in the Dene (Dutch for "valley"), the Cop Cot (Anglo-Saxon for "hilltop cottage") near Central Park South, and a similar, unnamed structure in the Ramble—have the aura of rustic pagodas. Their benches are carved with the

{92} *Opposite:* One of two pavilions adjacent to Belvedere Castle.

{93} *Left:* A view in spring, overlooking the Turtle Pond from Belvedere Castle; the irregular shoreline enhances the peaceful view.

{94} *Right:* The Turtle Pond, a wildlife habitat that's home to fish, frogs, and waterfowl as well as turtles, is a designated quiet zone, especially beautiful at dusk.

initials of previous sitters. Visitors to the Summerhouse can watch the joggers and bicyclists on the Park Drive to the west, or the playground to the east, with its own smaller version of the Summerhouse.

Almost any large boulder is a potential lookout point, an informal observatory. A Manhattan architect points out the beauty in the craftsmanship of steps carved by hand into the bedrock throughout the Park; the work is now more than one hundred years old and Park visitors are still climbing up these stairs but aren't wearing them out. He praises their well-proportioned angles; how the ratio of riser to tread works extraordinarily well, enhancing a fluidity of motion as climbers move from pathways to stairs. "You can enjoy looking at the Park, you don't have to watch your feet." A set of steps in a natural outcropping leading up to Pine Bank Arch near the southwest corner of the Park proves not only this point, but also the larger point that the more you look at Central Park, the more there is to see.

Summit Rock, at about 83rd Street near Central Park West, is the highest natural point in the Park,

slightly higher than Vista Rock. A snaking path with tree-branch handrails heads uphill along the southern edge of Summit Rock, leading into a stone stairway; a curving path from the east follows the arc of a stone wall on top. The crown is a mostly grassy area with a shelf of rock. Just below, stone benches and a terraced area provide a stage for impromptu or planned theater. Well before the area was landscaped, this place drew people: according to legend, in pre-colonial days Native Americans used this rock as a meeting place. These days, when no one is making use of the stone stage, people enjoy the lofty quiet at the top. Perhaps those who are drawn here to read, meditate, or daydream can hear some echoes of the past, of traditional expressions of respect and gratitude for the natural world.

An elevated area of the Park known as the Mount is interesting not only for its location on a hill above the Conservatory Garden, but for its centuries-old history. Today it's the site of the Park's composting efforts, a heap of leaves and branches with a view. In the 1700s, it was the site of a tavern, later renamed McGown's

{98} *Opposite:* A slope covered with bright yellow daffodils is an early sign of spring.

{99} *Left:* The Summerhouse has a commanding view, and is also a fine place for inner reflection.

{100} *Right:* For many artists, the Park is a source of inspiration.

{101} *Left:* This curved stair-case leads from the southern part of the Dene to the East Drive, across from the beginning of Literary Walk.

{102} *Right:* The walkways of the Ramble traverse the area on several levels, and in winter, when the trees are bare, the Lake and skyline become vivid background.

Tavern for its new owners, and the strategic road it was situated on was called McGown's Pass. In the late 1840s, the tavern was sold to the Sisters of Charity of St. Vincent de Paul; they built a thriving religious community known as Mount St. Vincent on the site. When the land was acquired for the Park, the Sisters moved to the Bronx. The buildings were used by Park officials and, for a short time, as residences for the Olmsted and Vaux families. During the Civil War the Sisters returned briefly to run a military hospital at the site: after the War, the building again became a tavern, and was eventually torn down in 1917.

Although there's no plaque marking the spot, George Washington passed through here during the Revolutionary War, when he led troops across the northern part of the Park en route to Harlem Heights, after losing the Battle of Long Island in Brooklyn. The British are thought to have erected a chain of strongholds near McGown's Pass, which they abandoned in defeat; the Americans rebuilt them for their own use in the War of 1812. The hilltop sites of Fort Clinton, Nutter's Battery (named for a nearby farm owner), and Fort Fish—

{103} **The Shakespeare Garden is built** into the rocky slope of a hill, with plants arranged on several terraces and walkways.

in the area between what is now 105th and 107th Streets, near Fifth Avenue—have no surviving structures. Now they overlook the Harlem Meer (Dutch for "lake") and the North Woods, but it's not hard to imagine them as lookout sites in the years before the East Side of Manhattan became a forest of apartment buildings, when it was still possible to see the East River from the Park.

An American flag flies over Blockhouse No. 1, the oldest structure in the Park, built in 1814. Standing on a high ledge in the clearing of a forested area at about 108th Street, uphill from Warrior's Gate, it's a simple square fort whose four thick walls are constructed of Manhattan schist and red brick. Today, plants and weeds grow out of cracks between the stones. Visitors who find this off-the-beaten-track relic can peek inside through its gated entrance. On its north side rises a dramatic view of the city.

The only observation point in the Park that requires no climbing and is accessible by elevator is the Iris and B. Gerald Cantor Roof Garden at the Metropolitan Museum of Art, open from spring through late fall.

{104} *Opposite:* The Blockhouse, a rugged stone shell that's a relic of the War of 1812, is located in the North Woods, north of the Great Hill.

{105} *Left:* A plaza on top of Summit Rock, with its stone terrace, that can be used as an amphitheater.

{106} *Right:* Cars passing through the park on the 65th Street transverse road are just below the grade level of the Park.

Here, the view includes sculptures—every year the work of one sculptor is highlighted—and a wide view of the Park just above treetop level, topped by a panorama of the skyline. A vine-covered pergola provides shade in this most refined of Park overlooks.

Add a bit more distance, and the views gain new perspective. From the windows and roofs of the surrounding buildings, the Park is a sharply defined rectangle of foliage, many shades of green in the spring and summer, turning to a palette of gold and red in the fall. Savvy tourists who stay in the hotels along Central Park South ask for rooms on high floors facing the Park; a room with a view on Fifth Avenue may even help ease a hospital stay. People who live across from the Park often arrange their furniture to bring as much Park as possible into their homes. They understand that every time you look out, something is different.

{110} *Opposite:* An open field dotted with evergreens on the west side of the Park.

{111} *This page:* A sundial is set amidst the plants and flowers in the multi-level Shakespeare Garden.

Water Views
{112-136}

FOLLOW ANY PATH IN CENTRAL PARK, AND BEFORE TOO LONG YOU'RE LIKELY TO ENCOUNTER A BODY of water. Olmsted and Vaux understood that water was an important element in creating the varied landscapes they envisioned, so they designed lakes of various shapes and fit them into the Park much like puzzle pieces. The four large lakes—the Pond in the southeast corner, the Lake in the West 70s, the Pool at West 101st Street, and the Harlem Meer in the northeast corner—all have pipes running under them, and are about as natural as the sea lions' water habitat in the Zoo. Not that the sea lions aren't comfortable in a place that feels like home, but their swimming hole is artificial.

Water, even when piped in as decoration, adds something luminous to the mix, at times reflecting the Park all around it like a mirror; it can be still as stone, or may ripple to its own rhythms. It's not unusual to see people standing along the shore of the Pool, staring at the water, mesmerized, or to encounter artists with easels and paints along the paths near the Pond, creating their own interpretations of the scenery.

In Central Park, water isn't used for drinking, the lakes are no longer used for ice-skating, and the only swimming is in the Lasker Pool at the North End. The waterways are home to fish, waterfowl, and all sorts of

{112} *Opposite:* **Although Olmsted and Vaux may not have envisioned the skyscrapers, the aim of their Greensward Plan was to create scenic landscapes like this idyllic view of the Lake, seen here on a late-fall afternoon.**

plants. Up at the Harlem Meer, visitors can borrow bamboo fishing rods, help themselves to bait, and try to meet up with some of the golden shiners, largemouth bass, bluegill sunfish, carp, and other fish. But since the Park has catch-and-release ordinances, none can be served as dinner. Recently someone made an unusual find in the Meer—an exotic caiman, a member of the crocodile family usually found in South and Central America. Now called Damon and ensconced in his own tank of water in the Children's Zoo, he probably had been someone's house pet, set free.

On the Meer's east bank, a small sandy patch leading down to the water is called "the beach"; the pigeons seem to enjoy sinking their feet into the sand. One late fall morning, when the plants around the water's edge are sparse, a metal drainpipe that's well-concealed most of the year, rises out of the water, a reminder of its origins. In the background, sounds of the Temptations fill the air, broadcast from loudspeakers at the Lasker Rink and Pool, which displaced a corner of the Meer when it was built in the 1950s. A row of seagulls, all looking

{113} *Opposite:* **The Dana Discovery Center faces out onto the Harlem Meer, with the skyline of 110th Street behind it.**

{114} *Left:* **Rowboats are available for hire at the Lake, adjacent to the Loeb Boathouse.**

{115} *Right:* **Natural rock outcroppings provide resting places close to the Lake.**

{116} *Left:* The Meer and the area around it was one of the last parts of the Park to be built; a swamp was transformed into the 11-acre Meer.

{117} *Right:* The Loeb Boathouse features an outdoor bar, facilities for outdoor and indoor dining, and an informal café inside.

{118} *Opposite:* In the Park's early years, the Lake when frozen was a very popular destination for ice-skating.

north, sit on the pointed rooftop of the Charles A. Dana Discovery Center, which stands in place of an old boathouse. Its design is a mix of Victorian and Alpine, and although it's completely new, it looks like it could have been designed by Vaux in a playful moment. From the exhibition hall on the main floor, visitors can sit on an Adirondack-style bench and look out through a broad picture window at one of the best panoramic views in the Park, encompassing the Meer, Duck Island, the Locust Grove, the North Woods, the buildings of upper Fifth Avenue, and more.

Shift to a winter afternoon when ice covers half of the Lake—the largest of the Central Park lakes—and the ducks waddle across it, with the same unsteady, slightly anxious gait that a human being might employ in the same situation. Watching them, a swan in the water, inches away from the ice, arches her neck and holds her wings at just the right angle, so that she appears to be wearing a tutu. A woman who calls herself "the substitute bird feeder" (filling in for a friend who is home sick) scatters bread crumbs and apologizes to the ducks

for getting there later than usual. Around the Lake, posted signs ask visitors not to feed the birds, but this New Yorker says her loyalty is with the ducks.

In warmer weather, the songs of the Park's gondolier can be heard above the clanking of oars and oarlocks aboard the rented rowboats. The striped-shirted gondolier is following a tradition that goes back to earlier days, when a Venetian-built gondola, presented to the Park in 1862, was available for rent. Back then, small ferry boats used to take passengers around the Lake, stopping at the Belvedere Terrace and at six other "stations." These days, renting a rowboat may bring to mind the scene from Woody Allen's *Manhattan* when he and Diane Keaton row together on the Lake. Their romantic moment abruptly ends when he dips his hand into the water and comes up with a handful of muck.

Four of the old ferry landings are still in place, including a rebuilt shelter at Hernshead, a peninsula on the western shore that's covered with daffodils in the spring. On top of a large boulder jutting into the Lake,

{119} *Opposite:* The detailed ironwork of the Ladies' Pavilion frames a striking view of the Lake and skyline.

{120} *Left:* Designed by Mould, the Ladies' Pavilion is a fanciful, colorful structure with finials on the roof.

{121} *Right:* A gondolier transports passengers around the lake on a Venetian gondola; there's no extra charge for his songs.

{122} *Left:* The bucolic scene is interrupted by the sound of oarlocks and, occasionally, other people's music.

{123} *Right:* The Loeb Boathouse was opened in 1954, replacing a Victorian structure on the Lake's eastern shore.

{124} *Opposite:* The Bow Bridge, with its 142-feet balustrade, is favored by bird-watchers, photographers, and romantics.

people read and stretch out on the jagged surface, looking a bit like the sea lions in the Zoo, who claim their pieces of rock to soak up the sunlight. Just beyond the outcropping, the Ladies' Pavilion provides shade in an ornamented Victorian-style shelter with cast-iron railings. First used as a streetcar-stop shelter at Columbus Circle, it was moved here in the 1910s to make room for a monument at Merchants' Gate. Hernshead is magical at that golden moment when day is turning to evening: to the southeast, the light-filled skyline is reflected with perfect symmetry on the glassy surface of the Lake.

One of the few Central Park bridges over water, the Bow Bridge is perhaps the most documented of the Park bridges. Named for its shape, it cambers gracefully across the Lake, connecting Cherry Hill and the Ramble. Designed by Vaux and Mould, it was completed in 1862. The shadow of its cast-iron balustrade projects a lacy pattern onto the wooden walkway, from which there's a clear view of both the East and West Sides of the city.

{125} **The Lake, stretching over 20 acres, is a signature view of Central Park, with the tree line and skyline in the background.**

The Lake can also be appreciated from inside the Loeb Boathouse at its eastern end. Although known for its restaurant with alfresco dining in warm weather, inside this building there's also a lesser-known, self-service café with a panoramic view. A mirror on the back wall reflects the cherry trees on the other side of the Lake, so visitors feel snugly surrounded by the Park. On winter mornings, it has the cozy atmosphere of a ski lodge: there's an active fireplace and waves of people who seem to know one another flow through the room. The earliest visitors are the bird-watchers, followed by the runners, then small groups of friends who walk through the Park together. Later in the day, baby-sitters and their charges, tourists, and maintenance workers pass through. The baker, proud of his muffins and of the "tremendous view," boasts that this is one of the most romantic spots in New York City. Most mornings he arrives by six o'clock. "It's quiet and I love to hear the different melodies of the birds."

East of the Boathouse and down a sloping lawn—or through the Trefoil Arch— sailors and yachtsmen

{126} *Left:* A detail of the cast-iron Gothic Bridge, designed by Vaux, near the Tennis Center and Reservoir.

{127} *Right:* The Lake is particularly mesmerizing at those times of day when the skyline seems perfectly reflected in the water.

{128} *Left:* Musicians entertain at the plaza adjacent to Georg Lober's sculpture of Hans Christian Andersen—here, holding a bouquet of balloons.

{129} *Right:* Sparrows gather as sunlight bounces off the Conservatory Water.

maneuver their boats from afar at the Conservatory Water, an oval pool used for sailing model boats. On a winter Sunday, two young boys can't help yelling commands to their boats, even though they hold the controls in their hands. In the Greensward Plan, Olmsted and Vaux hoped to build a formal garden with a glass enclosure here. That project was abandoned because costs were too high, but the name has remained (although it's also known informally as "the boat pond"). In the 1920s, model boat contests were held here, along with ice-skating competitions. Nearby, two bronze sculptures—José de Creeft's *Alice in Wonderland* and Georg Lober's *Hans Christian Andersen*—are popular sites; kids love to climb onto the mushroom where Alice is sitting or into Andersen's lap (he's holding a book). The area has been a storytelling mecca since 1956.

On the west side of the boat pond a telescope set up on a tripod points at a building on the corner of Fifth Avenue and 74th Street. Several bird-watchers hold vigil, their sights trained on a pair of red-tailed hawks who've nested on a curved window pediment, several floors up, since 1994. "They're Central Park celebrities,"

{130} Alice is joined by other Lewis Carroll characters including the Mad Hatter, White Rabbit, Cheshire Cat, and March Hare in this bronze sculpture by José de Creeft.

one of the friendly and devoted watchers points out, offering a view of the raptors. He explains that this is a rare opportunity to see them nesting in an open area, and that fellow hawk-watchers have witnessed them eating rats, making love, and hatching their eggs. The adventures of the hawks and their fans are documented in Marie Winn's book, *Red-Tails in Love*. The bird known as Pale Male has a four-foot wingspan, the man adjusting the telescope reports, as the hawk soars about forty stories high in the New York sky.

Mention the Reservoir and most people will associate it with running. That might have something to do with Dustin Hoffman's 1976 film, *Marathon Man*. The late Jacqueline Kennedy Onassis used to run here regularly and, after her death in 1994, the Reservoir was named in her memory. Built between 1858 and 1862, the pear-shaped Reservoir, raised above the level of the Park, is larger than any of the lakes. It's no longer used as a source of drinking water, and its future function is uncertain. (Of course, many New Yorkers have ideas about that, including building a boat basin, swim club, or an amusement park.)

{131} *Opposite:* This fountain on Cherry Hill features water flowing out of eight small flowers into bowls, topped with eight glass lamps and a golden spire.

{132} *Left:* The track around the Reservoir is well-traveled throughout the day by runners and walkers.

{133} *Right:* A chain-link fence separating the track from the Reservoir captures light in changing patterns.

{134} *Left:* **A polar bear in his tank at the Central Park Wildlife Center, better known as the Zoo.**

{135} *Right:* **A sea lion luxuriates in the sunshine, stretched out on a rock.**

Olmsted and Vaux imagined people wandering about on the Park's scenic paths rather than running in circles, but a lap around the Reservoir does offer the changing views they favored. A runner who circles the Reservoir several times a week says that he loves the sense of wide open space; just before dusk he likes to watch as the Park's lights, the luminaires, with their yellow glow, come on. Runners on the northern edge can also catch a glimpse of one of Vaux's most striking cast-iron bridges, Gothic Bridge, which arches over the bridle path leading to the clay tennis courts.

Back at the Zoo, snow monkeys and penguins also spend their days close to water. A fifth-grade boy on a school trip says the penguins are "awesome," his all-time favorites, and he thinks they're performing just for him. As the penguins jump off their ledge and into the water, he and his friend mimic the animals' movements, from their own imaginary body of water on the other side of the glass.

{136} The Conservatory Water, also known as the boat pond, reflects the Fifth Avenue buildings that overlook it.

Private Spaces
{137-161}

THE CENTRAL PARK LANDSCAPE LENDS ITSELF TO SOLITUDE. NEW YORKERS WHO WANT TO BE ALONE can find it throughout the Park, in off-the-beaten-track hideaways or well-traveled locations where the atmosphere is invariably serene. Nature itself offers a layer of privacy: the trees appear as curtains enfolded in light. And those who like their seclusion amidst company—in the spirit of writers who go to crowded cafés to be "alone"—can find contemplative spaces, a cocoon of privacy, even with people around.

The ingenious system of separate pathways, with their underpasses and overpasses, encourages every visitor to explore and enjoy the Park in his or her own way. Some seek a kind of privacy that has nothing to do with quiet. Every day, a drummer who plays at jazz clubs around New York comes to the Park to practice, trying out new ideas on his Nigerian bata drum. "I don't come here with other musicians," he says. "Then it would be a performance, not practice." He likes to play on a bench near the lawn-bowling field just north of the Sheep Meadow, but when there are people bowling there, he finds another place.

Nearby, the Wisteria Pergola is a not-yet-popular place, well-suited to writing poetry, studying, or just sitting. Time seems to be suspended in this narrow lane covered with wooden latticework, entwined with vines.

{137} *Opposite:* The West Drive runs above the Glen Span Arch, and a footpath passes underneath. Close to 102nd Street, the arch, made of large gray stones, is a portal into the wooded area of the Ravine.

In spring, wisteria blossoms in all shades of violet and lavender gracefully dangle, before falling to create a pastel carpet. The gnarled trunks look like weathered seats, too fragile to sit on. The area was created as a shaded overlook to the Concert Ground, where open-air concerts have been held from the Park's earliest days. The original cast-iron bandshell designed by Mould was replaced in the 1920s by a solid limestone version, named the Naumburg Bandshell. Lined with benches, the Pergola is now sandwiched between two concert venues; the Bandshell below and, to the east, the Rumsey Playfield, site of a summer music festival. During the morning and early afternoon, quiet pervades this most pleasant arbor, but many summer evenings include a musical interlude.

Olmsted and Vaux wanted visitors to the Park to be so immersed in their pastoral surroundings that they'd stop worrying about their urban concerns, at least for a few moments. It's as though they were prophetic, understanding the Park's therapeutic value, and not only for those people who could afford no other escape.

{138} *Opposite:* The pace is naturally slower in the Ravine, where a path runs alongside dense flowering shrubs and a bridge with a handmade wooden balustrade.

{139} *Left:* Many places in the Park can become private alcoves for reading and relaxing.

{140} *Right:* A gentleman finds his own use for the Naumburg Bandshell.

 Left: The Turtle Pond offers quiet moments for meditation.

{142} *Right:* Many musicians use the Park as their rehearsal studios, enjoying the acoustics and, for some, the audiences.

{143} *Opposite:* A stone path alongside bright azaleas leads to Wagner Cove with its wooden shelter on the Lake; a lamppost is a reminder of the city.

A corporate lawyer who often walks to work through the Park in a suit and tie says that his walks have helped him get over disappointments at work as well as a broken heart. "The deeper you go into the Park," he says, "the more remote your worries become."

The Park radiates a quality of healing. "I have a prescription from my doctor for Central Park," says a young woman who had spent time confined to a wheelchair and now comes to the Park every day to walk. She makes loops around the area of the Boathouse, returning there to rest. Another woman who often does yoga in the Park, practicing headstands next to a large rock that she can lean against, says that she likes the karma of the space, its bountiful peacefulness.

If you were doing a tour of mystical New York, the Ramble would certainly be one stop. Here, in this hilly, rugged, shady woodland with its stream, waterfalls, and bridges, nature appears to be at its wildest and most intriguing—although, like the rest of the Park, it's an artifact born of the planners' vision.

Meant as a place for ambling about, the Ramble has its own rhythms. The many byways, which occasionally rise on steps cut into the rock, create a maze-like pattern; even a Park guide says it's easy to get lost here, temporarily. Retracing one's steps, or following the same route on a subsequent visit, can be a challenge. Close to the western entrance to this area, Ramble Arch, made of rough stones, lends mystery: Without peeking, wanderers have no idea what's on the other side. Further east is the source of the Gill, a scenic pile of boulders above the pipe that supplies the stream running through the Ramble. Follow the Gill and you'll encounter bird-watchers, and very likely some beautiful birds as well, at the Azalea Pond; it's easy, even for a novice, to identify a brilliant cardinal.

The Ramble offers a series of vistas, some partially concealed. Pockets of light illuminate awe-inspiring still-life scenes, and from points like the Willow, a sunny cove with elegant willow trees leaning into the Lake, the Bethesda Terrace comes into sight. Views of an earlier Ramble, with more open space and more sculpted

{144} *Opposite:* The Loch, as it runs through the wooded Ravine; a Conservancy-led tour through this area is aptly titled "Manhattan Adirondacks."

{145} *Left:* The Huddlestone Arch in the Ravine, built in 1866, is made of huge boulders gathered in the Park held together simply by gravity.

{146} *Right:* A waterfall in the Ravine is a bucolic spot that feels very distant from the urban streets not far away.

{147} *Top left:* **A burst of goldenrod, plentiful in the Wildflower Meadow.**

{148} *Bottom left:* **A tree surrounded by asters.**

{149} *Right:* **Pink and white hollyhocks rise tall and straight above a rustic fence.**

landscaping, are captured in an 1862 album of lithographs drawn from nature by G. W. Fasel. In its present state, the Ramble is still beautiful, but probably more tangled and overgrown than Olmsted and Vaux had intended.

Less well-known than the Ramble, and farther north, the Ravine feels even more distant from urban life. No lampposts line the pathways. With its low elevation—below the general grade of the Park—the view of the skyline is lost. This may be the quietest place in the Park; the main sound comes from the Loch (Scottish for "lake"), built as a long, narrow lake but now more of a creek that babbles and cascades over rocks in several places on its way to the Meer. This picturesque landscape within the North Woods is less dense and less crowded than the Ramble. Even on weekends, it seems like a personal sanctuary.

To the east of the Loch, a meadow overgrown with wildflowers hosts a convention of hummingbirds and butterflies. The Huddlestone Arch, built in 1866, is the northern gate to the Ravine. Constructed of large boul-

{150} A flowering empress tree overlooking the concourse on top of Cherry Hill.

116

ders, using neither mortar nor metal, it nevertheless supports the Park Drive that runs over it. At the southern end of the Ravine, near the Glen Span Arch, two grand red oaks, within an oval created by two converging paths, are among the oldest trees in the Park. When a group exploring the Loch emerges through the Glen Span Arch, climbing up out of the Ravine toward the Pool, a hawk is waiting there, perched in a black locust tree, as though this meeting were planned.

Private places can also be invented. The terrace surrounding the octagonal Chess and Checkers House in the southern end of the Park, with its small checkerboard-topped tables, has the feel of an outdoor café, but strictly "bring-your-own." Several regulars do use the place for its intended purpose and have made it their chess clubhouse. Groups of players sit outside for hours every afternoon, alternately playing, watching others play, and talking. The most serious players bring timers and their own covers for the tables; sets can also be borrowed from the nearby Dairy.

{151} *Opposite:* A clearing in the Ravine with a pair of stately, historic red oaks.

{152} *Left:* A spread of asters dominates this lush field.

{153} *Right:* Small groups also find places in the Park where they can feel as though they are alone.

 Left: Busy chess tables surround the octagonal brick Chess and Checkers House, built on a large outcropping called the Kinderberg, or Children's Mountain.

 Right: At the Turtle Pond a solitary reader chooses sun over shadows.

{156} *Opposite:* In the 19th century, children enjoyed fresh milk at the Dairy. The granite building and its wooden loggia were erected in 1870.

Possibilities for serenity present themselves all over the Park, indoors as well as outdoors. While the Victorian Gothic-style Dairy has a public role as an exhibition space, visitors' information center, and gift shop, its back table is an undiscovered refuge for readers. A cabinet of Park-related books is available to the public for on-site reading, and there may be no better place for studying *The Papers of Frederick Law Olmsted* than at this table, sitting in front of a window with a fine view looking down a hill and past a large outcropping, toward the Pond and Wollman Skating Rink.

Especially in winter, the Tropical Zone in the Central Park Wildlife Center (better known as the Zoo) is conducive to thinking and observing. There are no cages here: colorful paradise tanagers swoop down, close enough that they can be encountered eye-to-eye. The multi-leveled, steamy environment also hosts monkeys behind glass. Animal sounds reverberate, but this urban rain forest still has a certain peacefulness—that is, when it's not being shared with groups of schoolchildren. Upstairs, after walking through a curtain of

car-wash-style hanging rubber strips, visitors enter a small world of darkness, where day becomes night, and they can observe bats, ants, and all sorts of other exotic creatures, behind glass.

For those whose solitary experience is enhanced by enjoying refreshments along with a view, the Zoo has its Leaping Frog Café; guests at Tavern on the Green can look out onto the Sheep Meadow; and at the back of the Metropolitan Museum of Art, the Petrie Court's café tables face out onto the Park through a tall wall of windows. Here visitors can sit, surrounded by sculpture, and watch the ever-changing scene, a kind of street theater. The shadow of the building shifts slowly across the stage, as people play their unwitting, walk-on roles: a young boy chases a white ball and his mother chases him; a man folds up a blanket he's been sunbathing on and hangs it over his bicycle; a young girl does cartwheels, unaware that she has an audience.

{157} *Opposite:* Mist envelops the Sheep Meadow in early spring.

{158} *Left:* A patch of flowers and greenery in the northern end of the Park.

{159} *Right:* Designed as a garden of peace, Strawberry Fields has plantings sent by countries around the world, as identified on this plaque.

{160} *This page:* Wisteria blossoms dangle like bunches of grapes, their vines tangled around the wrought-iron pergola.

{161} *Opposite:* Behind and above the central area of the Conservatory Garden, the ornate Wisteria Pergola forms an arc; May is the peak month for the blossoms, in shades of lavender, pink and violet.

Gatherings
{162-186}

VISIT CENTRAL PARK ON A SUNDAY MORNING, AND THE THEME IS MOVEMENT; PEOPLE RUNNING, WALKing, bicycling, horseback riding, roller-skating, and pushing strollers on the East and West Drives. On the ball fields, depending on the season, people play soccer, football, softball; others toss Frisbees or practice tai chi in the open meadows. Elsewhere, players compete in handball, tennis, croquet, and lawn bowling. All that energy infuses the air.

Although the people running and riding alongside each other don't necessarily know one another and might never converse, there's an abounding spirit of community, a strong sense of Central Park as a shared treasure. Some folks will stop and spend an hour or so watching a softball game with players they don't know, or chatting with other people seated nearby whom they're likely never to meet again. And then there are smaller communities, like the roller skaters who dance to pop music east of the Sheep Meadow, the exercise classes of mothers with strollers, the model boat racers and chess players, groups that have been gathering informally in the Park for years.

{162} *Opposite:* In warm weather, the Sheep Meadow is the site of simultaneous energetic activities as well as lounging; the flat green field appears larger than the 15 acres it takes up.

 {163} *Left:* The rocky slope in front of the Dairy is a popular gathering place.

{164} *Right:* A young man takes time off from bicycling to practice gymnastics in the plaza near the Naumburg Bandshell.

{165} *Opposite:* Friends relax in the grassy area adjacent to the terrace overlooking Wollman Rink.

The Park is also alive with romance and the search for it. In 1905 a football player named Morris Friedlander was running down a Park field during the Harlem championship game and ran right into Bertha Persky, who was watching the game. They later married, as reported in Rosenzweig and Blackmar's *The Park and The People*. More recently, a solitary man rode a bicycle-built-for-two, trying to meet a woman who would pedal along with him; he may still be trying.

People wandering around the Park in groups may be on one of a number of tours available through the Urban Park Rangers, the Conservancy, or various private organizations. A Ranger wearing a tan Stetson leads one group around the North End after giving a lecture on winter survival skills. He describes the Rangers as peace officers and stewards of the Park, as well as educators, and notes that he's been called on to help a swan being chased by a dog, to rescue other animals, and to give directions to tourists.

"Wildman" Steve Brill, a naturalist and Park lover, organizes very different tours. Wearing a safari helmet,

{166} The Park's playgrounds are often the sites of children's birthday parties; balloons mark the spot.

he leads participants on hikes in search of edible greens and herbs—and they fill plastic bags with the potential ingredients for a meal. Described in the press as a weed maven and "the man who ate Manhattan," he says that Central Park is a great place to forage, because of "its varied habitats and the combination of wild and cultivated, native and exotic plants." Depending on the season, his groups might come across field garlic, chickweed, winter cress, root vegetables like burdock and wild carrots, sassafras, seeds of a Kentucky-coffee tree that can be brewed for decaffeinated coffee, wild blackberries, mulberries, June berries ("one of the best-tasting fruits in the world"), wild allspice and, of course, mushrooms.

The people who arrive at Belvedere Castle by 7:30 A.M. for a bird-watching walk led by Urban Park Ranger Dr. Robert DeCandido are used to the swooshing noises their leader makes: he imitates the calls of specific birds, hoping they'll answer him back, and often he's successful in locating them. "Central Park is one of the few green spaces in the area on the migration flyway," he says, explaining why the Audubon Society describes

{167} *Left:* An exercise group uses an open field on the west side for practice.

{168} *Right:* Newly-fallen acorns, another edible product of the Park, add a bit of color to the grass.

{169} *Left:* Young men park their bicycles before taking off for a ride around the Park Drive.

{170} *Right:* Musicians and martial artists find their own corners of the park to practice and perform; sometimes it's the same corner.

{171} *Opposite:* Many areas of the Park are well-suited for birdwatching; egrets are frequently sighted, along with two hundred other species.

it as one of the best birding spots in the United States. Dr. DeCandido, who holds a doctorate in ecology, notes that between 175 and 200 species are identified in the Park every year, including migratory birds and year-round residents. Among his great bird-watching moments in Central Park are sighting a golden eagle, and observing a few thousand broad-wing hawks soaring overhead.

In the words of a guide for the Conservancy who is herself a recent arrival in New York, "Central Park is like the I-95 for birds. Who knew?" The best times for seeing the greatest variety of birds are during the spring migration, when warblers, hummingbirds, orioles, summer tanagers, and herons appear; and fall, when chickadees, nuthatches, and water birds abound. Winter is also an opportune time; it's easiest to spot birds when there's no foliage to camouflage them.

Following Dr. DeCandido on a January morning, a group of ten men and women—all carrying binoculars, some wearing multi-pocketed vests—wander slowly toward the Locust Grove on the west side of the Great

Lawn, where a red-headed woodpecker has been spotted. Darting back and forth between an oak and a locust tree, the woodpecker finds storage space for the acorns he's collecting in the grooves of the locust bark. The group is also thrilled to see an immature red-tailed hawk near the 86th Street transverse, and at the Reservoir they watch some canvasback ducks. They head back to the Duck Pond, through the Ramble to the Azalea Pond, where a white-breasted nuthatch dines at a bird feeder hung during winter months, and then to the Boathouse, where the bird register is kept. Birders record their experiences and note the birds they sighted, designating the locations using their own code names, like Warbler Rock, in a blue loose-leaf notebook; some pages are simple lists, while others read like poetic briefs.

A group of French-speakers from Paris and Brittany meets every afternoon to play pétanque, a game similar to the Italian lawn-bowling game of boccie. Mostly men, they have claimed a flat clearing in a wooded area south of the Heckscher Ballfields as their court, and depending on how many people show up, sometimes they

{172} *Opposite:* Christian Eratin's *Eagles and Prey*, cast in Paris in 1850, is the oldest-known sculpture in any New York City park; it was moved to Central Park in 1863.

{173} *Left:* Young women use the pergola of the Chess and Checkers House as their dance studio.

{174} *Right:* Near the Scholar's Gate, at Fifth Avenue and 60th Street, a portrait artist at work.

have two games going at once. They toss small steel balls, aiming to land them as close as possible to an even smaller wooden ball called a cochonnet ("piglet" in French). After a particularly good shot, a teammate is likely to shout "Encore!" a term also frequently used just a few blocks away, at Lincoln Center.

Foreign languages and accents can always be overheard in Central Park, but especially in the days leading up to the New York City Marathon, held each year in early November, as people who have traveled from all over the world arrive to compete in the race, and often train in Central Park. Although the route of the Marathon now goes through all five boroughs of the city, with its finishing line at Tavern on the Green, the race was initially staged entirely in Central Park. For the first five years, from 1970 to 1975, runners looped around the Park four times; in 1970, fifty-five people finished the race, and the winners were given recycled bowling trophies at a simple awards ceremony. In 1976, under the direction of Marathon co-founder Fred Lebow, who served as president of the New York Road Runners Club for twenty years, the 26.2-mile race was

moved out of the Park. Today, there are 30,000 participants and two million spectators, and the event is given major international press coverage. Lebow died in 1994: his contribution is commemorated by a life-size statue, situated below the Reservoir track, near the East 90th Street entrance to the Park. The bronze Lebow is wearing a baseball cap and a sweatshirt, and is looking at a stopwatch.

A Tennis Center with thirty clay tennis courts northwest of the Reservoir is crowded throughout the season with players and spectators. When tennis was first permitted in the Park in the 1880s, players volleyed on a grassy meadow where the courts now stand; they were paved in 1914. At the nearby North Meadow Recreation Center, there are handball courts. North of the Sheep Meadow, on one of the greenest patches in Central Park, players can sign up for a formal game of lawn bowling or croquet. Evenings, in spring and summer, the ball fields host competitive softball leagues organized by profession—law, theater, and publishing, among others. Weekends, Little League teams take over the fields. But league play isn't the only game in town—

{178} *Opposite:* **Soccer is played on regulation fields as well as on makeshift areas on the Park's lawns.**

{179} *Left:* **Unicycles, vintage bicycles, and tandem bicycles can all be seen in use in the Park.**

{180} *Right:* **City permits are required to play on the Park's clay tennis courts.**

{181} *Left:* Roller skating is popular on the park drives as well as in Wollman Rink (during summer months only).

{182} *Right:* An area west of the Mall is the base of a group of people who dance on roller skates to the beat of recorded music.

there are also impromptu ball games going on all over the Park.

Walking through Central Park offers encounters with not only unexpected vistas, but also unusual events. The Parks Department and the Central Park Conservancy plan all kinds of programs that vary from year to year; there have been celebrations of Burmese New Year and winter festivals. For Halloween, there may be a parade at the Meer, followed by a display of floating jack-o-lanterns lit with candles, while Bethesda Terrace is transformed into a country field of hay bales and pumpkins. Annual attractions include the summer concerts on the Great Lawn given by the New York Philharmonic and the Metropolitan Opera. On those evenings, music is a connecting thread among the thousands of listeners seated on blankets that form a patchwork stretching across the entire Lawn and beyond. Over the years, Barbra Streisand, Diana Ross, Garth Brooks, Paul Simon and others have also given concerts, attracting huge crowds.

Most visitors to Strawberry Fields have music on their minds. The open meadow, named for the title of

{183} The tile mosaic dedicated to the memory of John Lennon was a gift of the city of Naples, Italy.

one of the Beatles' best-known songs, and planted with trees and shrubs from all over the world, is dedicated to the memory of John Lennon, who lived and died in the nearby Dakota apartments. A circular mosaic of Italian tiles arranged in geometric patterns around the single word, "Imagine"—the title of Lennon's most famous song in his post-Beatles career—has become a kind of shrine, a touchstone for memories, a must-see stop for tourists. People pay their respects, often leaving flowers and memorabilia behind.

The day that George Harrison died in 2001, Strawberry Fields drew hundreds of the late Beatle's fans. Some sat grieving in silence in a ring just outside of the memorial mosaic, which was covered with photos, letters, sheet music, roses and other flowers, lit candles, incense, and fruit. Others formed another circle around four guitarists who played "All Things Must Pass" and other Beatles tunes, as the crowd sang along. Many brought cameras to this place of solidarity and remembrance, creating new memories as they relived old ones.

{184} *Opposite:* Horse-back riders on the bridle path pass underneath Pine Bank Arch.

{185} *Left:* The scenic bridle path runs for more than four miles, following several loops.

{186} *Right:* Horses can be rented at a nearby stable and lessons are available in the Park.

Changing Vistas
{187-212}

SOME EARLY SUMMER EVENINGS AT TWILIGHT, THOUSANDS OF FIREFLIES CREATE A BOULEVARD OF flickering tiny lanterns adjacent to the Swedish Cottage Marionette Theater. The next night they might be gone. In Central Park, no two days are alike. Between nature's constant process of growth, and the changes wrought by the human endeavor of caretaking, the landscape and the views are unceasingly renewing and reinventing themselves.

"It is a favorite resort at all seasons of the year, and he who visits at each is confident that he has seen it in its most beautiful time." Henry Cleveland's words, published in 1870 in an essay titled "The Central Park" in *Appleton's Journal*, could have been written today. Certain views of the Park—a lane of lilac trees in blossom, so fragrant that admirers carry the scent away with them, or a Black Locust tree, its angular branches piled high with fresh snow—are likely to elicit either silent awe or strings of superlatives.

On fall afternoons, it's not uncommon to see backpacks dropped in a heap, and their young owners engaged in a game of tag, or a pick-up game of football at the base of Cedar Hill. All around are bursts of golden leaves, with touches of deep red and burnt orange; a red-headed toddler blends in with the general color

{187} *Opposite:* A festival of light at dusk, with bright white snow highlighted by the glow of the luminaires.

{188} *Left:* Joggers use a path they've created, called a desire path, en route to the Reservoir track.

{189} *Right:* The Pine Bank Arch, with its ornate cast-iron handrail, connects two large rock outcroppings.

scheme. One of the joys of fall is walking through ankle-deep fallen leaves and hearing the rustling, crinkling sounds. During October, Monarch butterflies appear on their migration route south, congregating in garden areas, such as the Wildflower Meadow in the North End of the Park.

When they are bare, the London Plane trees seen throughout the Park seem particularly sturdy and state-ly; their bark peels off and the lower trunk looks as though it's splashed with the gray, drab green, beige and cream patches of a camouflage design, while the upper trunk and spreading branches stand out in their light coloring against the November sky.

Beginning in late fall, ice-skaters have their choice of Wollman Rink at the southern end of the Park and Lasker Rink on the northern end. On Christmas Day at Wollman, a skating guard wearing a Santa hat says that he's never aware of the buildings surrounding the Rink when he skates. But he did notice a hawk flying over the Rink a few weeks before. Early mornings, advanced skaters pay a premium rate to skate when they have the

{190} A maple tree in its autumn radiance is a solitary shock of red in the open field.

Rink virtually to themselves. An outdoor observation gallery provides views of the skaters as well as the Hallett Nature Sanctuary and the Pond.

At dawn after a snowfall, the Park is magical; the fields look like they're covered with clouds. Icicles dangle from trees and the eaves of wooden shelters; snow clinging to fences creates striking geometric patterns. With its bright whiteness, snow imbues the Park with an aura of purity and peacefulness. The view from the Sheep Meadow could be of a rural New England landscape, except for the skyscrapers. Even a few inches of snow brings out a playful spirit in New Yorkers, as parents and children head to the hilly areas of the Park with all sorts of colorful, makeshift sleds. Cross-country skiers form their own tracks in the Sheep Meadow and alongside the Park Drive.

Bright yellow daffodils are among the first flowers to make their springtime debut in the Park, usually in March. Thanks to generations of gardeners, the ongoing blossom show runs through September, with forsythia

{191} *Opposite:* A winter afternoon in the Ramble, with the towers of the San Remo on Central Park West in the background.

{192} *Left:* Thousands of skaters use the Wollman Rink daily in winter.

{193} *Right:* Generations of New Yorkers have learned to skate in Central Park.

{194} *Left:* A path underneath a trellis leads into the northern, French-style section of the Conservatory Garden.

{195} *Right:* Each day in spring, the Garden appears a bit different.

{196} *Opposite:* Many shades of pink distinguish the Park in springtime.

in April, azaleas in May, roses and mountain laurel in June, bottlebrush buckeyes and day lilies in July. Ragweed flourishes in August, goldenrod in September. In the sun the colors are radiant; on drizzling mornings the flowers still have an opalescent glow. Rain brings a certain coziness to the Park. Fewer people are wandering then, but the dog walkers and other stalwarts make eye contact, knowing that they're sharing something extraordinary.

"In the trees the night wind stirs, bringing the leaves to life, endowing them with speech; the electric lights illuminate the green branches from the other side, translating them into a new language," E.B. White writes, about stopping off at a concert in the Mall on a summer evening in his 1949 essay, "Here is New York." "On the bench directly in front of me, a boy sits with his arm around his girl; they are proud of each other and are swathed in music . . . . In the wide, warm night the horn is startlingly pure and magical."

In spring and summer, picnickers lug baskets or shopping bags loaded with feasts, simple or lavish, to the

Park. Some people bring books and blankets and head for one of the open meadows, where they enjoy sun-bathing in New York City's alternative to the beach. In warm weather, when the pace may be slower, many visitors enjoy taking in the scenery from the almost 9,000 benches that are placed throughout the Park. Some of the wooden and wrought-iron benches are modeled after those made for the 1939 New York City World's Fair. There are also simple wood-and-iron benches without armrests, and a wood-and-concrete version. Near the Naumburg Bandshell on the Mall, benches with ornamented wooden backs are based on Vaux's original designs, and wooden benches made from curving locust or cedar branches are found in places like the Ramble and the Shakespeare Garden. In earlier times, some benches had mudguards in front of them to protect women's skirts. Seating in the Park was a source of controversy in 1901, when the Parks Commissioner consented to a plan to rent chairs for a nickel apiece. Immediate protests ensued, and angry park visitors refused to pay. The policy was reversed and since then, everyone sits for free, anywhere.

{197} *Opposite:* Tavern on the Green, lit up with tiny colored lights at night, looks enchanting.

{198} *Left:* In the 1930s, the sheepfold was converted into a restaurant, and elements of the original Victorian structure are visible.

{199} *Right:* Tavern on the Green is located just inside the Park at 67th Street.

Through the Central Park Conservancy, donors can select a bench—noting its number on the back of the top slats—and adopt it. Engraved plaques may commemorate the life of someone who was enamored of a particular view, the location of a romantic moment in the Park, or just someone who loves the Park.

A vendor who sells hot dogs and pretzels on the Park Drive near Literary Walk reports that people often stop to ask him questions about the Park—and the most frequent query is for directions to Balto. They're looking for the bronze statue of the Alaskan sled dog that in 1925 led a team bringing emergency medical supplies through a great blizzard to Nome, Alaska. Balto toured the United States and was present in Central Park later that year when the statue, located near the Willowdell Arch, was dedicated. Many kids now know Balto's story from a 1995 animated film about the heroic dog.

Children who love animals enjoy the Zoo, officially known as the Central Park Wildlife Center, and its smaller interactive annex, the Tisch Children's Zoo, where they can feed sheep, cross a brook over a bridge of

lily pads, and observe the golden pheasant strutting about with her iridescent red and orange colors. Some New York sparrows manage to make their way through the netting above and share the bird's food. "Interlopers," a Zoo volunteer says, shaking his head, but smiling.

At the Friedsam Memorial Carousel, kids of all ages can choose to ride on one of the fifty-eight colorful, hand-painted horses or one of two chariots. There have been several carousels at this site, and this one was built in 1908. According to legend, the first carousel, opened in 1870, was run literally by horsepower: a horse and a blind mule in the basement kept the merry-go-round turning.

Most of the twenty-one playgrounds are close to the Park's perimeter, visible from street level and near the entrances. Just north of the Metropolitan Museum of Art, the Ancient Playground has equipment with Egyptian themes, and at the Safari Playground, on the west side, kids like climbing on the many rhinos. Each playground seems to have its own community of regular visitors: clusters of nannies, baby sitters, and parents

{203} *Opposite:* Frederick G. R. Roth's life-size bronze sculpture of the Alaskan sled dog Balto, here looking out over the Park.

{204} *Left:* A covered archway connects the Zoo's major buildings and exhibit areas, grouped by climatic zones.

{205} *Right:* The distinctive organ music of the Friedsam Memorial Carousel fills the surrounding area.

group together, as though continuing conversations from the previous day. Heckscher Playground, near 61st Street on the west side, was the first equipped playground, added to the Park in 1926 and named for philanthropist August Heckscher, whose gift provided swings, merry-go-rounds, slides, and other equipment. Today, a climbing structure kids like to call "the castle" connects to the adjacent Umpire Rock, a large outcropping of Manhattan schist that's also popular for climbing. One young child in a puffy jacket insists that hanging upside down on the swings provides an amazing view, too.

"Central Park is not just a landmark for New York City, but for the country," says Barry Lewis, an architectural historian who co-hosted a 2002 television documentary about Central Park with David Hartman. Noting that it was the first American urban park in a country with no prior tradition of urban parks, he adds, "We were lucky. It's not just a major public park, but a brilliant design." About Central Park today, he says, "It's a revelation to see it so beautiful."

157

In many ways, Central Park looks different than it did in the 1800s, but it continues to be the breathtaking refuge that Olmsted and Vaux conjured up. Their signature is forever imprinted on the land. The Park is an urban paradise, an oasis, an open-air sanctuary. Even people with no religious leanings agree that it is a soulful place. It's a place to explore the road not taken, and discover something new when exploring it again.

{209} *Opposite:* In autumn, fallen leaves carpet the steps leading up to the Chess and Checkers House.

{210} *Left:* A winter view of the Lake and skyline from the Balcony Bridge.

{211} *Right:* A corner of Bethesda Terrace, early-summer flowers in the sandstone urn.

{212} No two bridges or
arches are the same.
Like the Park around them, they
are works of art.